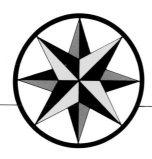

EXPLORING SCIENCE THROUGH ART

EXPLORING SCIENCE THROUGH ART

BY PHYLLIS KATZ

FRANKLIN WATTS 1990 A FIRST BOOK
NEW YORK LONDON TORONTO SYDNEY

Library of Congress Cataloging-in-Publication Data

Katz, Phyllis, 1946–

Exploring science through art / Phyllis Katz.
p.   cm. — (A First book)
Summary: Demonstrates how many forms existing in art are
taken from natural phenomena and suggests art projects using
simple motifs from nature.
ISBN 0-531-10890-2
1. Art and science—Juvenile literature.   2. Nature (Aesthetics)—
Study and teaching—Juvenile literature.   3. Art—Study and
teaching (Elementary)—Juvenile literature.   4. Science—Study and
teaching (Elementary)—Juvenile literature.   [1. Art and science.
2. Nature (Aesthetics)]   I. Title.   II. Series.
N72.S3K38   1990
704.9'43—dc20   89-38621   CIP   AC

To the memory of my father
In whose butcher shop I first learned some anatomy
While classical music wove in and out of the lambchops
And chicken legs.

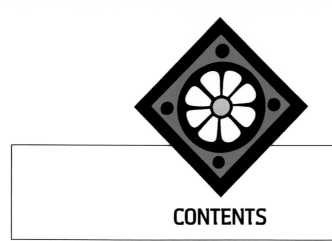

CONTENTS

ARTFUL SCIENCE
OR
SCIENTIFIC ART?

ART OR SCIENCE?

When you look at a rainbow, what do you see and what do you think? Are the colors always the same and in the same order? Why is there never a square or triangular rainbow? Why do rainbows usually appear late in the afternoon as a rain comes to an end? Why are some of them high and bright and others low and faint?

You can see rainbows in the sky only when you are standing so that the sun shines through the water in the air at an angle that breaks up the sunlight in the same way as a prism. That happens most frequently when the sun is low in the sky in the afternoon. You can try making your own rainbow by controlling the angle of the water from a garden hose.

< 9 >

You can see a rainbow because the world works the way it does. Discovering how the world works and predicting how new things will work are part of what you call "science." But you enjoy rainbows because they are beautiful. People write songs, tell stories, and paint pictures about them. That is "art."

Though we study art and science as separate subject, they have a lot in common. Both scientists and artists take a closer look at the world around them and try to tell us what they see. Both can do experiments to find out what happens when things are mixed together or separated according to their plans.

You learn what is beautiful from the people around you. When your parent says, "What lovely flowers!" you are learning what they think is beautiful. Since what you see is something you learn, people who grow up in different places, with different experiences, can be taught to see differently from you. People from all over the world have taken the materials they have found where they are and made the things they needed. They have wanted them to be beautiful as well as useful.

ART IN OUR SCIENCE

A bridge only has to connect two pieces of land and be strong. But when engineer John Roebling designed the Brooklyn Bridge over 100 years ago, he made it both

< 10 >

The Brooklyn Bridge in New York City
combines usefulness and beauty.

beautiful and useful. Often once we have made something we want to experiment with the ways to make it beautiful. We take new science inventions and find ways to make them into art. Electronic synthesizers make new musical sounds. Computers create pictures from tiny dots in a screen. We seem to need beauty in our lives as much as we need food, clothing, and shelter.

THE EYES HAVE IT!

We see well because our eyes are very good at taking in information about shape, distance, movement, and color. We also see well because many nerves send pictures from our eyes to our brains where they make sense to us. Our brains are "tuned" to quickly make sense of what our eyes see. We are taught to pay attention to some things more than to others. We also learn to expect to see some things in a certain way. How is that?

For example, take a paper plate of any size and cut two sections of the rim (arcs) to exactly the same size. Place one on top of the other and trim them so that you are certain that they are duplicate shapes. Now lay them flat on a table with one above the other. Does one look smaller? Your eye/brain compares the inner curve of the upper plate rim to the outer curve of the lower plate rim and "tells" you that the upper piece is smaller because you have been trained to "believe" that a line that fits inside another one indicates a smaller item. Often you

< 12 >

will see what you expect to see or even what you want to see.

FROM EYES TO
BRAIN TO HAND

Artists understand how trained eyes work. They can make you think, for example, that you can see miles into the distance on a flat piece of paper.

Try this: Take a plain piece of paper and draw a horizontal line across it about a third of the way down the page. This will be your horizon. Now pick a point on your horizon. This will be the "vanishing point." Start from that point and draw two lines toward the bottom of the page, spreading them apart. What do you have? It could be a road leading off into the desert. Maybe it's a river coming out of the mountains. What happens when you start the "vanishing point" at the bottom of the page? What happens if you change the space between the lines? When you go outside, see if this is the way a road looks to you.

Although this seems quite simple, people did not know how to draw with *perspective,* as you just did, until the period of history we call the Renaissance (about A.D. 1400–1600). Those who studied art and geometry uncovered the mathematics of how to show distance. They were so excited about the "trick" that many of the paintings during that time show it over and over.

< 13 >

*Above: This early American painting shows
no understanding of how to display distance
on a flat surface. Facing page: The meeting of the
lines at the "vanishing point" shows understanding
of the mathematics of perspective in this
16th-century painting by Raphael.*

MORE HINTS
TO THE BRAIN

You have also been trained to take many "sight clues" from the way light hits an object.

Try this: Draw a circle on a piece of paper. Take a ball and shine a flashlight on it from different distances to see what happens to the shadows that you make on it. Now, draw shadows on your circle in the same place you see them when you shine the flashlight. Those shadows give our brain a signal that we should think of the circle as a ball.

We depend on other clues to tell us size in art as well as in science. Often, you tell size by putting something new next to something you would expect another person to know. A gemstone, in a book on rocks and minerals, will be shown next to a penny. If you live in the United States and you know from your experience exactly how big a penny is, that will tell you how big the gem is. If you are from another country and don't know the size of U.S. coins, then the penny won't help you at all. Seeing has a lot to do with what you already know.

Try this: Look around you and think about what objects would make good size references. You could make a list and then mark your list for those things that would make sense to almost anyone and those that would be understood only by certain people or groups of people.

< 16 >

Figure 1. All of these circles are drawn the same size, but look different when you see the other objects around them.

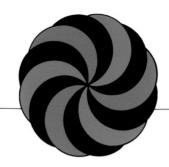

WHAT'S IN THE SHAPE?

IN THE ROUND

Shape is one of the first characteristics you notice about an object whether you approach it for science or for art. Shape tells you something about structure and what you can expect from the object. You already know that a ball should be able to roll and that a cube will not. Look around you for examples of circles, spheres, and cylinders. You will see bubbles, trees, flowers, rings, tubes, jars, tires, wires, buttons—and how many other things? Why do you find variations of the circle or sphere in so many forms?

Try this: Cut a pipe cleaner long enough to form a circle 2 inches (4–5 cm) in diameter. Now bend it into a triangle and lay it over the circle. Does the triangle en-

< 18 >

close more space than the circle? Bend the same piece of pipe cleaner into a square. Does the square enclose more space than the circle? Try other shapes. Which shape gives you the most enclosed space?

Try this: Can you blow a square bubble? Take a pipe cleaner and bend it into a square with enough handle left over to hold onto it. Dip it into sudsy water or bubble solution and blow. What shape is the bubble? The liquid is "pulling" to be as small as possible and the air inside the bubble is pressing out evenly in all directions. The shape you get is the only one possible. You can try forming all sorts of single blowing wands and compare the bubble shapes.

A WORLD OF WHEELS

It would be hard to look at circles in science and art without thinking about the wheel. That unknown ancestor of yours who first rolled stones or logs began a long history of applied science, or technology. Movies, for example, wouldn't be possible without the wheels and gears that spin the film past our eyes.

Try this: You can begin to understand how movement is made possible from single pictures by putting together the following simple wheel. Draw a circle about 8 inches

< 19 >

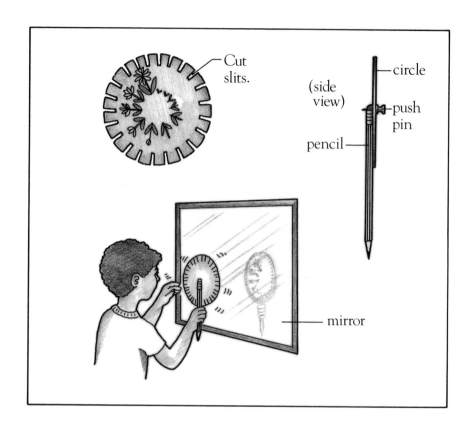

*Figure 2. Construct this wheel
to see a "moving" picture.*

(20 cm) in diameter on a piece of tagboard. Starting about an inch in from the edge, draw about a dozen pictures in a slow-changing series, such as a flower growing up and blooming. Cut 1-inch (2.5 cm) slats, about a quarter of an inch (.6 cm) wide. Attach your circle to a pencil with a pushpin and spin it around until it spins

< 20 >

easily. Stand in front of a mirror and hold the circle up so that the pictures face the mirror. Spin the wheel and look through the slats. The pictures move past your eyes so quickly that one of them blends into another and you believe that you see movement. Once you've mastered simple drawings, try something more complicated.

'ROUND THE
FLOWER GARDEN

Have you noticed that flowers are almost all "in the round?" While they have certain basic parts that they need, they also have an enormous number of variations on the theme of the circle. Scientists have, in fact, used circular pictures called "floral diagrams" to show flower parts as they are studied.

Try this: Flowers are classified in many ways, depending on their parts, their symmetry (balance of shapes), and when and where they bloom. Dissect a few flowers from your garden or a store to identify the parts. Draw what you see to make your own floral diagrams. You can also classify the flowers in a simple way by taking data (counting and making notes) about the petals. How many of your flowers have an even number of petals and how many an odd number? (Do you know the old game of "She loves me, she loves me not"?) How does the number of petals affect the symmetry of the flower?

< 21 >

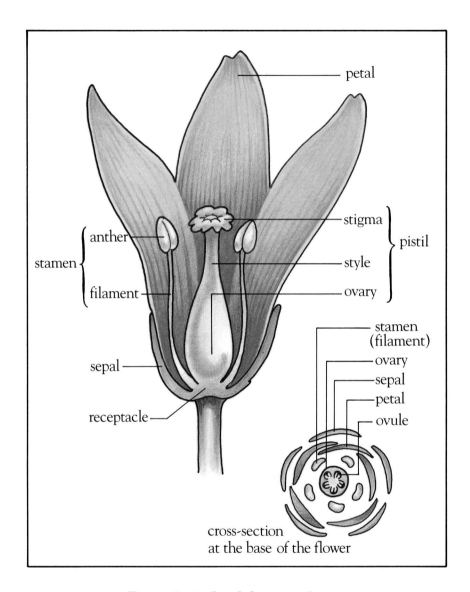

petal

stigma

pistil

anther

style

stamen

ovary

filament

stamen
(filament)

ovary

sepal

sepal

petal

ovule

receptacle

cross-section
at the base of the flower

*Figure 3. A floral diagram shows a
flower's parts "in the round." Dissect
a flower and draw your own floral diagram.*

These variations in nature have also been interesting to artists. In the late nineteenth and early twentieth centuries, some tried out a style called Art Nouveau. The artist looked closely at plants and animals and repeated the design and the colors.

Try this: Find a live flower or photograph of a simple flower that you like. Draw it in a repeat pattern in the Art Nouveau style. Try coloring the same drawing with different colors. Artists often do these kinds of patterns when they prepare for a much larger piece.

Art Nouveau design with repeating flower patterns

< 23 >

ALL SQUARED AWAY

While circles are one of nature's ways of getting the most for the least, straight-sided shapes have the advantage of being able to sit neatly side by side. When the midwestern and western parts of our country were divided for farms and ranches in the nineteenth century, it was done in squares and rectangles. Can you find other examples of square and rectangular shapes around you?

Aerial view of fields laid out in a patchwork.
Why are the shapes rectangular?

< 24 >

In your survey of squared shapes, you may have noticed bricks, cinder blocks, and other building materials. What are the advantages and disadvantages of building with this shape?

Try this: Design a simple building on paper, then try to construct it out of sugar cubes and glue. How does science play a part in solving construction problems?

THE ETERNAL TRIANGLE

Any two points can be connected to form one straight line. Any three points that are not in a straight line can be connected to form a triangle.

Try this: With a paper and pencil, experiment by making sets of three points and connecting them. Use a protractor to measure the inside angles of your triangles. The markings on the protractor are in degrees. Add up the number of degrees of the three angles of one of your triangles. Now do this for several more. What do you find?

Have you watched any new homes go up? Triangles are used in building to prevent wobbling. This is called "cross bracing." Some furniture is also constructed using cross bracing.

< 25 >

*Figure 4. What happens when you form
triangles in cross-bracing?*

Try this: Cut five strips from the light cardboard. Attach three of the strips together, using two brass paper fasteners, and rotate them into a "U" shape. You can rotate the legs of the "U" in either direction. This is not too stable. Now attach the fourth strip across the two legs. Start by securing it under one of the paper fasteners already in place and then along the opposite leg using another paper fastener. Attach the fifth strip from the opposite corner and along the opposite leg. Does it wobble easily now?

< 26 >

A pyramid is the three-dimensional shape you get when all sides are triangles of the same size on a square base. Which is a stronger shape, a pyramid or a cube?

Try this: Cut six plastic straws in half and slip a pipe cleaner through each piece. Twist the ends of the twelve straw pieces together to form a cube. Twist six pieces together into a pyramid shape. Push on the cube. What happens? Push on the triangle. What happens?

A pyramid will support weight better than a cube.

< 27 >

Look at the cut end of a corrugated cardboard box. What do you find? Many bridges use the strength of the triangle in their construction to support the roads on which we cross.

Try this: Use toothpicks and glue to build a bridge. Does it make a difference if you use flat or round toothpicks?

PUT THE HEX ON

The regular hexagon ("regular" meaning all sides the same length) is another strong shape that we find in nature. We have borrowed it for our art too. The bees make their hives using this shape and it is one of the basic shapes of the molecules of living (or formerly living) things. The chemical benzene, for example, has a hexagonal structure. Snow crystals are also hexagons.

The hexagon encloses the greatest amount of space of all regular geometric shapes that can fit side by side like puzzle pieces, without any space between them. The inventor R. Buckminster Fuller (1895–1983) designed a structure called a "geodesic dome," using hexagons. It is sturdy and easy to put together.

A geodesic dome makes use of hexagonal shapes.

< 28 >

Try this: You can measure and cut out regular hexagons and tape them into a geodesic dome. How would you divide the inside of such a home into rooms? Think about how many rooms you would want, how you would get to them, and how you would add inside floors.

Try this: "Grandmother's Flower Garden" is the name of a quilt pattern that uses hundreds of hexagons to form its design. Try making a small version of one of these quilt blocks in colors that please you. Create the shape with thin paper and then make a sturdy cardboard version to use in cutting out your fabric pieces.

SYMPATHY FOR SYMMETRY

When you decide whether you find an artwork pretty, your mind and eyes work together in many ways that you may not even think about. One of these is a sense of balance or symmetry in the shapes. Perhaps this is because people are pretty symmetrical. There is an imaginary line down your middle, from the center of your forehead. On either side you have an eye, an arm, an ear, and so on. But do you really look as if you were cut like a folded paper doll and opened up?

Try this: Take your most recent school photo or other good full-face close-up picture of yourself and a mirror

< 30 >

"Grandmother's flower garden" is a traditional
quilt pattern of hexagons.

with a straight edge that you can easily hold in your hand. Place the picture on a flat surface and put the edge of the mirror along your nose in the photo, down that imaginary center line. Hold the mirror so that you can easily see the reflection of this half of your face doubled. Is the full face made by the half picture and its reflection the same as your photo? The same as you think of yourself? Try this on others.

< 32 >

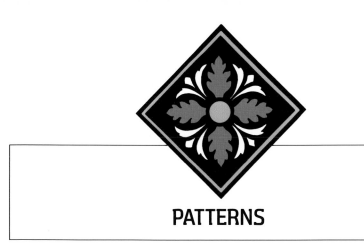

PATTERNS

Much of what science has done has been to classify what we find in the world. You expect that things in the same group will do the same things. Classification helps you to predict or *hypothesize* the ways things work by showing patterns. Artists also show patterns of design and movement. So strong is the need to find patterns that you will find them when there are only suggestions. Look at the shapes below. None of them are the ones you know as alphabet letters. But you see letters because your brain wants to sort out a pattern.

Figure 5.

< 33 >

A pattern repeats. It has a rhythm. Look around you with your mind on patterns. There are obvious patterns in wallpaper and floor tiles and more subtle patterns in shells, stones, the food we eat, even the way we talk.

TIME IN A JAR

Layers of rock show us the history of the earth in striped patterns of stone put down over millions of years. You can see these on highways that have been cut through rock.

Try this: To make your own colorful layers, you'll need a jar and enough fine white sand to fill it, some food coloring, small zip-top plastic bags, and toothpicks. Sketch out a plan for your layers on a piece of scrap paper and then mix drops of food coloring in the plastic bags until you get the colors you want. Add the sand and shake the bag until the sand is colored the way you want it to be. Start layering the colored sand according to your plan. You can create more intricate designs by using a toothpick to push parts of the layers down into previous ones as you work.

Rock layers of the
Grand Canyon in Arizona

< 34 >

MILLIONS
OF SNOWFLAKES

Many snowflakes are hexagons. Their size depends on
how wet it is and what the temperature is high up where
they are formed.

W. A. Bentley worked at his "snowflake-collecting"
hobby for fifty years. You can't hold a snowflake, because the warmth of your hand will melt it. Bentley col-
lected samples on a cold blackboard and snapped pictures of them through a microscope. Since water is
colorless, he had to plan his lighting very carefully.

< 36 >

Try this: You can decorate your windows with simulated snowflakes. Start with a circle of paper. You'll want paper that's fairly thin like typing paper or tissue paper. While white is closer to natural snow, you can take artistic freedom and use other colors too. Fold your circle in half and then in thirds. You can make creative cuts at the point, and all along the edges. When you unfold your design, you will have a hexagonal pattern, like a snowflake.

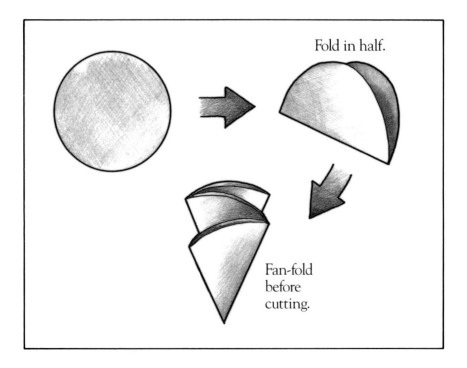

Fold in half.

Fan-fold before cutting.

Figure 6. Cutting snowflake hexagons.

< 37 >

TESSELLATING
IS TERRIFIC

In your search for patterns around you, you probably came upon a certain type of repeat pattern shape that left no spaces. You often find these in bathrooms or kitchens, which are tiled in simple squares, but you may have noticed fancier designs in a house of worship, subway station, or other old building. Shapes that fill a surface without spaces are called *tessellations.*

The use of identical tiles to cover a surface began a very long time ago, probably as a way to make a strong, waterproof surface. There are tile roofs in China that are over two thousand years old. The insides of many Islamic mosques are covered with tile patterns, also called "mosaics."

Mathematicians have been interested in tessellations for almost as long as artisans have. They call the process of filling a surface with figures that fit together "tiling the plane." A plane is another word for surface and "tiling" tells us that these patterns were first used for practical floor and wall tiles.

Try this: Design your own tile pattern. Combine shapes to make them tessellate. It's also fun to create a tessellation pattern in black and white lines. Make copies and see all the different ways it can look by varying the colors you use to color them in.

< 38 >

A tessellation design fills a space with no gaps.
This print is by artist M.C. Escher.

Try this: Can you think of two related objects and connect them through a tessellation pattern? Try raindrops and roses for starters.

Try this: Tessellation shapes make challenging puzzles. Unlike jigsaw puzzle pieces, which are all different, tessellation shapes are all the same. Your only clues come from the pictures printed on the surface. To see what this means, take a magazine picture and glue it to a piece of light cardboard. Use a hexagon pattern to trace tessellating hexagons over the entire back of the picture. Cut out all the hexagons, mix up the pieces, and try to put the picture back together.

THE ARTFUL COLLECTOR

Collections allow you to assemble samples to observe, compare, and enjoy. How you collect requires knowledge of science facts. The patterns in your display collections show your understanding of classification and your artistic talent.

Some items, like leaves, are fragile. Others can't be moved, like tree bark and interesting information on old tombstones. To collect these patterns, we can use the simple method of rubbing.

Try this: You can experiment with different papers and rubbing materials. Pencils, crayons, and charcoal can all

< 40 >

A gravestone rubbing (Wakefield, Massachusetts, 18th century)

pick up good details. Rubbing is also a great way to collect special coins that you can't own, if the owners will allow you to rub the coin surfaces.

Try this: Large boxes of crayons have silver, gold, and copper colors. You can use them to do rubbings of coins, or look for something else special to "collect" in this way.

< >

While it is perfectly acceptable to simply lay out and label whatever you collect, there are other creative ways to display what you've got.

< 41 >

Try this: Why not make your collection an artful pattern? Create your own patterns from nut shells, seashells, coins, beads, leaves, feathers. You can lay them out and move them around until you like the design and then glue them in place.

ALL DRIED UP

Water is an important part of all living things. The patterns in plump, wet things are different from shriveled and dried up ones.

The process of losing water is called *dehydration.* Adding water is called *hydration.* Since water supports living things, including those that cause decay and rot, dehydration is one way of preserving. You know that dried fruit lasts longer than fresh fruit. Dried starch, such as pasta, can last for years, compared to moist starch, such as bread.

Try this **(this activity should only be performed with adult supervision):** Take a large, firm apple and peel off the skin. Weigh the apple. Have an adult carve eyes, a nose, and a mouth into the apple with a knife. Put it on a paper towel in a cool, dry place. Check it and weigh it each day for about two weeks. It is ready to make into an apple-head doll when it is hard and brown. You can use a scale to determine how much of its water weight it has lost each day. This is an art that is done

< 42 >

peel apple   carve features

yarn

dowel

pipe cleaner

dried
"apple head"

*Figure 7. How fast does water evaporate from a sponge?
From an apple? You can make your own apple-head doll.*

quite well by craftspeople in the southern Appalachian Mountains in the southeastern United States. You can push a 6-inch-long dowel stick ¼-inch wide into the bottom of the head to support it. Use this as the beginning of a doll. Pipe cleaners can form the arms and legs. Yarn, cotton, or a doll wig can be used for hair. You can even sew a body and clothes. Stuff it firmly and you have a unique, "sculptured" piece.

We can preserve flowers for study and pleasure by dehydrating them carefully. Since water adds softness and flexibility to living things, dried flowers will be more delicate and fragile than fresh flowers, but they will also last longer.

Try this: Besides the flowers you want to preserve, you will need cornmeal and borax **(caution),** both available at the supermarket. They act as drying agents which pull and absorb the water out of the flowers. You'll also need a flat container with a cover, deep enough to "bury" your flower (or several of them). Mix enough equal amounts of the cornmeal and borax to fill your container. Put a layer of the mixture into the container, then place some flowers gently in so that none of their parts touch. Cover with another layer of the mixture. Cover the container and put away in a dry place for about three weeks. Carefully lift out the flowers after this time, clean them up with a cotton swab, and arrange in a bouquet or other display.

< 44 >

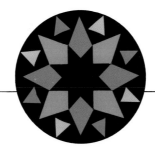

TOOLS AND MATERIALS

Having the right tool or material is very important in getting the result you want. A brush is not just a brush. Paint is not just paint. Could you imagine trying to paint the walls of your house with watercolors and a toothbrush?

MAKING AN IMAGE

When you try to take an idea from your mind and make it so that others can see it, you are creating an "image." If you are painting a picture, you must consider your idea, how you will put it down, what it is put down with, and what it is put down on. You may also want to think about how long you want it to last, how it will be displayed, and how it will be lighted. Each of these things you consider is called, in science terms, a *variable,* because you can change, or vary it.

< 45 >

When you do a science experiment, you try to look at only one variable at a time so that you can be reasonably sure you know what you are really testing. For example, if a marking pen gives you a fine line on a piece of dry paper and if you try that same pen on a different kind of wet paper and it smudges, you don't know if the smudging is due to the quality of the paper or to the wetness.

Try this: Find several types of paper: tissue paper, construction paper, typing paper, or brown bags. Cut them into test pieces. Now gather several types of drawing or writing tools: pencils, pens, markers.

Try each type of writing tool on each type of dry paper, using a simple straight line or a repeating design. What are the differences in the way the papers receive the lines?

Try this: Take another sample of each of the types of paper and dip them quickly into a pan of water. To compare the results easily, draw again on each piece of paper in the same order as the first time. You will see that some of your pens, pencils, and markers are water soluble (they dissolve in water) and some are insoluble. You have also seen that the different papers each allow for different amounts of spreading or "bleeding." You can mount your experiments as a collage, if you like.

< 46 >

SOLUBILITY AND ART

The fact that some things mix with water and some don't is the basis for a number of art techniques with which you can experiment and create lovely things.

Try this: Fill half a clear jar with water. What will happen when you add a tablespoon of vegetable oil? Cover the jar and shake. What happens? Try the same with shortening, butter, and other items, to test for their solubility.

< >

Now that you know something about solubility, try these techniques:

Simple resist: Use vegetable oil, a plain white candle, or a white crayon to draw a simple design on paper. Then use watercolor paint and brushes to "wash over" the design.

Marble paper: Fill a dishpan about two-thirds full with clean, cool water. Gently squeeze a small amount (about a tablespoon) of several colors of thin oil paint or liquid acrylic paints onto the water surface and swirl them with a brush or other tool. Carefully place a piece of white paper on the surface of the water and lift off the design. Put your new paper design on several layers of newspa-

< 47 >

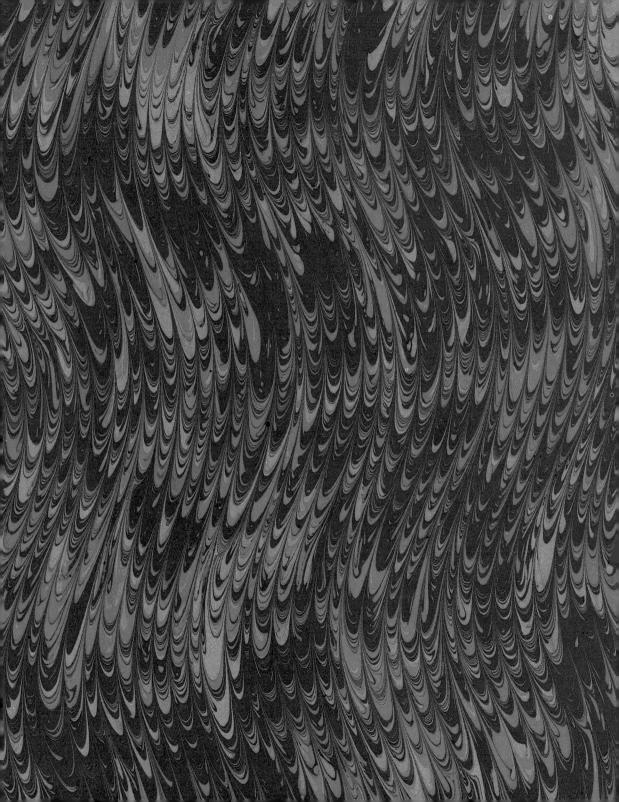

per to dry thoroughly. This takes practice, but the results make fancy wrapping paper, book covers, and anything else where decorative paper is useful.

Batik dyeing: This technique of putting designs into fabric originated in Indonesia. **It will require some adult help.** You know that water and wax will not mix. It follows then, that if you make a design on fabric with wax and then dye the fabric, the color will change only on the part of the fabric that is not waxed. You'll need to melt some candles or buy some paraffin wax. Use inexpensive brushes to "draw" with wax. You can also use cookie cutters (as stamps), sticks, or special tools called "tjanting" tools from an art store. **Warming and working with liquid wax is tricky, so ask for help.** Wash and dry a plain cotton fabric to get out any chemical coating (called sizing). Start with a piece of all-cotton fabric about 12 inches (30 cm) square and experiment with designs. It is easier to work if you stretch and tack the cloth to a board.

To dye the fabric, follow the instructions for a cold-water dye (hot water will melt the wax design away). Start with a light dye color. After dyeing, dry thor-

Marbelized paper design

< 49 >

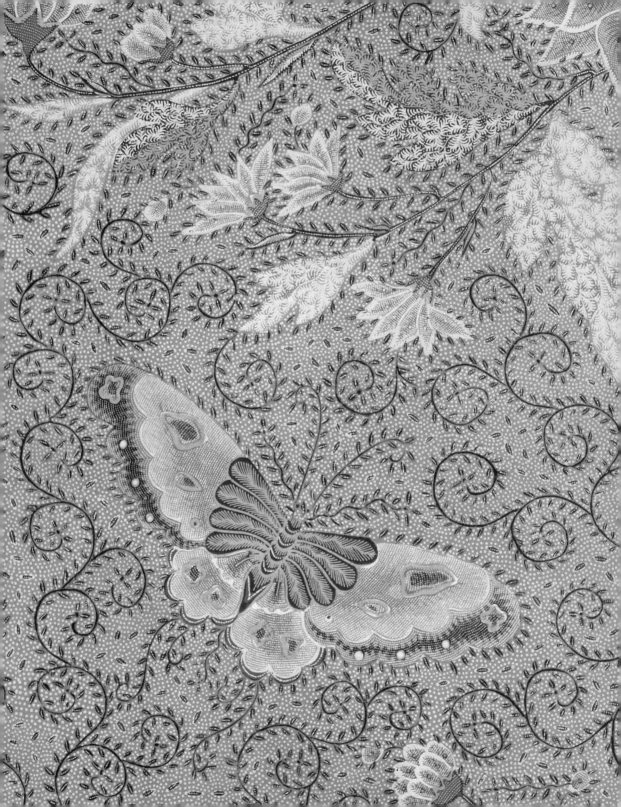

*You can create your own batik fabrics. Facing
page: A traditional Indonesian batik design.*

oughly, and if you like, dye again in another shade after
putting wax on the parts of the first color you want to
save. When you are finished with dyeing and your piece
has dried, you remove the wax by ironing the cloth,
wax side down, on layers of newspaper, until the wax
has melted out. The "cracked" design is special to batiks. You can frame your batiks or use them for pockets,
patchwork, dinner napkins, or other cloth projects.

< 51 >

Wrap string or rubber bands around tightly.

one tie-dye pattern

Figure 8. Technique for making a tie-dye shirt.

Tie Dye: Rubber bands and strings are also insoluble in plain water. The designs are different from what you can do with batik because you're not controlling a drawing tool. Instead, the limits of tying challenge you to new experiments with design. Wash and dry a piece of cotton fabric. Use rubber bands or string to tie up "bunches" of the fabric tightly. There's no wax to melt here, so you can use hot- or cold-water dyes. What do you notice about tie-dye patterns and how do they differ from batik?

DYEING TO KNOW

Dyeing is a very old technique for decorating fabric. There is evidence from India, China, and Persia that people dyed fabrics thousands of years ago. The colors to dye fabrics originally came only from flowers, trees, roots, and leaves. Today, many dyes are invented from processed chemicals. You can make your own dye colors from the things that are available in your garden or the grocery.

Try this: Here are three easily found items and the colors they will produce:

Yellow onion skins	yellow
beets	red/purple
spinach	green

< 53 >

1. Chop up vegetable or flower.

2. Boil in water and 3 tablespoons washing soda (available in supermarkets) for about an hour. (Check to see that there's always water.)

3. Pour out through a strainer so you'll have dye without bits of debris.

4. Dye cloth. Add vinegar and salt to help set the color.

Figure 9. You can make your own dyes using onion skins, beets, or spinach.

To make your dyes, just chop up the flowers or vegetables and boil the pieces in about a quart of water with 3 tablespoons of washing soda for about an hour. (**Do this with adult supervision.**) Use a glass or enamel pot. (Metal pots can react with the items to change the colors—or the pots!) What difference will the amount of water make? Add ½ cup vinegar and a couple of tablespoons of salt to help "set" the dye color. If you experiment with different amounts of water (to equal amounts of chopped-up material), you can make a color chart of the *intensity* (strength) of the colors you made.

Try this: To dye fabric, you need to know something about cloth. Get two pieces each of all-cotton, all-wool, and a polyester-blend fabric. Cut them each to exactly 12 inches (30 cm) square. Wash three pieces in hot water and three pieces in cold water. Allow them to dry on a line, flatten them out, and measure them again. What have you found? You may have noticed labels on your clothing that tell you how much "shrinkage" to expect after washing, so that you can judge what size to buy. This experiment shows you what "shrinkage" is. You have also washed out any of the chemical finish, or sizing, on your fabric and are ready to use it to dye with your homemade dyes.

Once you have used these natural dyes on your fabric samples, you can do another experiment on "fad-

< 55 >

ing." Take two dry samples of the fabric with the same color. Place one in a bright, sunny window and another on a shelf in a closet that gets no sun. Check on them after a day, a week, a month. What do you see? Do some colors fade faster than others? Do some fabrics hold color better than others?

INK

Inks were already in use by 2500 B.C. in the Chinese and Egyptian civilizations. They were first made by mixing the soot left after burning oil in lamps into a kind of gum or glue. This soot is called "lampblack." It is an almost pure black carbon pigment. Ink sticks were dipped into water and used to write. Through the years, inks have been made from many different pigments in solutions. These include indigo (dark blue from plants), sepia (a dark brown fluid from an octopuslike animal), dragon's blood (a dark red palm-tree fruit liquid), cochineal (red from certain dried female insects), and other animal, plant, and mineral substances. When the water or other solvent dries out, the pigment is left as the image.

Baby food jars with lids are good for storing ink. Mix inks with plastic spoons and throw the spoons away. Label your inks and keep them away from young children. Following are the ingredients for several types of inks.

< 56 >

Invisible ink: Use diluted milk or lemon juice with a fine brush or fountain pen. Experiment with how much water to add so that your writing is invisible when it dries, but turns readable brown when it is held up to a light bulb. Both milk and lemon juice come from living things. They have a lot of carbon in them. A warm light bulb gently burns off your ink fluid and leaves the carbon behind— just like the soot that was used in the early inks. **Be careful not to burn yourself or the paper on the hot light bulb.**

Vitamin power: Mash and dissolve an "iron" vitamin pill in a cup of strong (not herbal) tea.

Smoothie: Into a package of any cloth dyeing powder (from the supermarket), mix a small amount of rubbing alcohol to dissolve the powder. Add a half cup of glycerin (sold at drugstores) to thin it out.

Nice to the nose: Mix one tablespoon of liquid detergent with one tablespoon of oil of wintergreen. Add two tablespoons of vinegar and 5 tablespoons of turpentine. Use artists' oil paint to color the mixture the way you want it. Mix this all together.

Easy: Mix enough water with cloth dyeing powder to make it thin enough to use as ink.

< 57 >

While you have fun using and/or mixing up the inks and drawing with them, you can also keep in mind these questions:

Is your ink the "permanent" kind or is it water soluble? You can use a permanent ink to make up your own personalized t-shirt.

How long does it take for your ink to dry? Newspaper inks must dry very quickly as thousands of miles of papers shoot rapidly off the presses. Artists may prefer slower inks to smudge for effects. Try writing with different inks on one kind of paper. See how many seconds each type takes to dry. Change paper types and see how this changes drying time.

How much do your inks "feather," or spread out from the line that you draw on a given paper? Use a magnifying lens to take a look. Some artists like to wet a strong piece of paper and get that feathered look on purpose. Try that out for yourself.

How do your inks compare to commercial inks? Try some pens from your home or inks available at your school or an art store. Commercial inks often have many chemical additions to keep them from clogging, drying too quickly or not quickly enough, or getting gummy.

< 58 >

ENDLESS FUN,
ENDLESS EXPLORATION

If you have enjoyed this book and tried some of the experiments in it, you already understand how science and art blend together. Remember, the nature of true experimenting is that you don't know exactly what will happen.

You have only just begun. The artist in you needs to understand the way the eye, the mind, the hands, and the materials of art work. The scientist in you needs understanding and skill. Both science and art require imagination.

Can you imagine the cure for a disease or the shape of a space vehicle? Could you design shoes for underwater living? There is some of the artist and some of the scientist in each of us as we grow into the future.

< 59 >

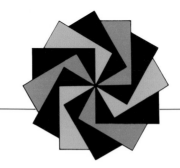

FOR FURTHER READING

Allen, Janet. *Exciting Things to Do With Color,* J. B. Lippincott, New York, 1977. This book, which uses lots of color, has over a dozen colorfully illustrated ways to explore the use of color.

Allison, Linda, and Katz, David. *Gee Whiz,* Little, Brown, Boston, 1983. Part of a series of large paperback books that have lots of good drawings and funny cartoons that talk about some serious subjects.

Barr, Beryl. *Wonders, Warriors and Beasts Abounding, How the Artist Sees His World,* Doubleday, New York, 1967. If you are interested in how artists have seen their subjects, this book has many good pictures of art from museums.

Frazier, Beverly. *Nature Crafts and Projects,* Troubador Press, San Francisco, 1972. Blends science and art by using nature "finds" to create attractive projects from woods to the seashore.

Holiday, Ensor. *Altair Design,* Pantheon, New York, 1970. A coloring book developed by a British biologist who likes geometry as a hobby. It has eight basic designs printed several times each. The many ways in which each can be colored in allows for many results from one pattern. Have fun!

< 60 >

Moore, Lamont. *The First Book of Architecture,* Franklin Watts, New York, 1961. Takes you all over the world with clear pictures of many buildings where people work and live. Along the way you see how shape and materials, art and science are blended.

Munari, Bruno. *From Afar It Is an Island,* World Publishing Co., New York, 1971. By examining very close up pictures of stones from an island, this book combines geology and imagination.

Sattler, Helen Roney. *Recipes for Art and Craft Materials,* Lothrop, Lee & Shepard, New York, 1973. Organized by types of art and craft materials; contains dozens of useful recipes to try out.

Seidelman, James E., and Mintonye, Grace. *Shopping Cart Art,* Collier Books, New York, 1970. Art materials and projects from the supermarket.

White, Laurence B., and Broekel, Ray. *Optical Illusions,* Franklin Watts, 1986. Is what you see what you are looking at? Read this book to find dozens of optical illusions.

< 61 >

INDEX

< 62 >

< 63 >

ABOUT THE AUTHOR

Phyllis Katz is director of the Hands-on Science Program in Rockville, MD, an after-school program for children (grades pre-K to 6) that stresses awareness of "science in your life." She lives in Silver Spring, MD with her husband, Victor, a mathematics professor, and their three children Sharon, Ari, and Naomi.